Costumes

by Lola M. Schaefer

Consulting Editor:
Gail Saunders-Smith, Ph.D.

Consultant:
Terry Kuseske
National Council for
the Social Studies

Pebble Books

an imprint of Capstone Press
Mankato, Minnesota

1

Pebble Books are published by Capstone Press
818 North Willow Street, Mankato, Minnesota 56001
http://www.capstone-press.com

Library of Congress Cataloging-in-Publication Data
Schaefer, Lola M., 1950–
    Costumes/by Lola M. Schaefer.
    p. cm.—(Fall fun)
    Includes bibliographical references and index.
    Summary: Photographs and simple text describe various costumes, including a
lion, a witch, and an angel.
    ISBN 0-7368-0104-9
    1. Children—Costume—Juvenile literature. 2. Children's clothing—Juvenile
literature. [1. Costume.] I. Title. II. Series: Schaefer, Lola M., 1950– Fall fun.
TT633.S28   1999
391—dc21   98-22678
                                              CIP
                                              AC

Note to Parents and Teachers

This series supports units on fall celebrations. This book describes
and illustrates several kinds of costumes. The photographs support
emergent readers in understanding the text. Repetition of words
and phrases helps emergent readers learn new words. This book
introduces emergent readers to vocabulary used in this subject area.
The vocabulary is defined in the Words to Know section. Emergent
readers may need assistance in reading some words and in using
the Table of Contents, Words to Know, Read More, Internet Sites,
and Index/Word List sections of the book.

Table of Contents

4

Costumes can have tails.

Costumes can have spots.

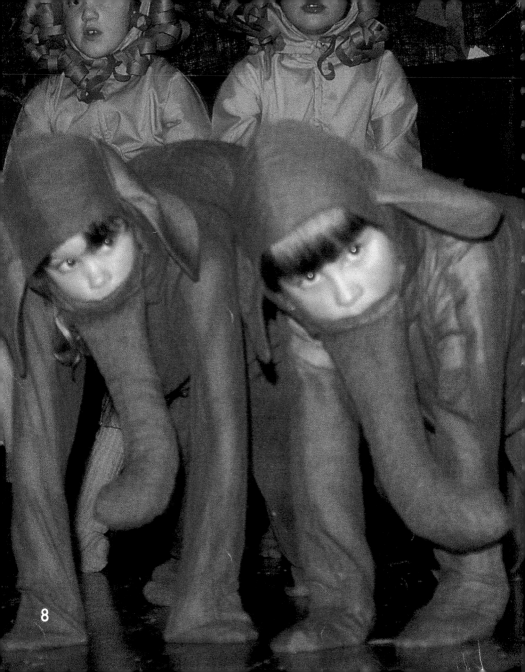

8

Costumes can have trunks.

Costumes can have manes.

Costumes can have stripes.

Costumes can have capes.

Costumes can have hats.

Costumes can have wings.

Costumes can be fun.

Words to Know

cape—a coat that ties around the neck and has no sleeves

costume—clothes people wear to hide who they are

mane—thick hair around the face and neck

trunk—the long nose of an elephant

Read More

Casey, Moe. *Dress Up.* The Most Excellent Book Of. Brookfield, Conn.: Copper Beech Books, 1997.

Hershberger, Priscilla. *Make Costumes!: For Creative Play.* Art and Activities for Kids. Cincinnati, Ohio: North Light Books, 1992.

Owen, Cheryl. *My Costume Book.* Boston: Little, Brown, 1995.

Wilkes, Angela. *Dazzling Disguises and Clever Costumes.* New York: DK Publishing, 1996.

Internet Sites

Costumes
http://www.netfix.com/poptart/costume.htm

The Halloween Costume Page
http://members.aol.com/nebula5/hallocst.html

Halloween Crafts and Costumes
http://www.bconnex.net/~mbuchana/realms/halloween/h-make.html

Index/Word List

be, 21
can, 5, 7, 9, 11, 13,
  15, 17, 19, 21
capes, 15
costumes, 5, 7, 9, 11,
  13, 15, 17, 19, 21
fun, 21
hats, 17

have, 5, 7, 9, 11, 13,
  15, 17, 19
manes, 11
spots, 7
stripes, 13
tails, 5
trunks, 9
wings, 19

Word Count: 36
Early-Intervention Level: 3

Editorial Credits
Martha Hillman, editor; Clay Schotzko/Icon Productions, cover designer;
  Sheri Gosewisch, photo researcher

Photo Credits
Doris Van Buskirk, 8
Gary A. Conner, 1, 16, 18
Photo Network/G. M. Brod, 4
Photri-Microstock/Lani Novak Howe, 10
Ting Lee, 12
Unicorn Stock Photos/Robin Rudd, cover; Les Van, 6; H. H. Thomas, 20
Victor Englebert, 14